The Social decline of the oystercatcher

This is a re-issue of Sue Vickerman's second poetry collection which first appeared in 2005, the manuscript having won Biscuit Publishing's 2003 International Poetry Competition. Sue went on to serialise the biographical trilogy of her fictionalised alter ego 'Suki' on the website sukithelifemodel.co.uk and she has also published a novel, *Special Needs*, and three further poetry collections, the latest being *Adventus*.

Sue's most recent projects have been translations of poetry and prose, mainly from German, including *Twenty Poems by Kathrin Schmidt*, and Schmidt's short story collection, *It's over. Don't go there.* Sue's works-in-progress include a filmscript, a further collection of poems, and a fictional tale about a literary translator's rocky path.

suevickerman.eu

About this collection

A breathless, breathtaking collection, nature *au naturel*: poetry refracted in the prism of her beacon eye, as effortless as a fulmar's flight… Birds given tongue and tangy taste… This riotous palette of colourful, heartfelt, sharply poignant, piercingly topical experience [is] a glorious achievement.

the late Magnus Magnusson

This is passionate, laconic poetry of a distinguished kind. Vickerman is best at the very exact landscape poetry which suggests, and sometimes defines, the emotions with which it is associated. But her versatility is such that she is also brilliant at interiors, like 'Tate Gallery, Turner's unfinished room', aural events ('Hearing about John Lennon') and even that bizarre thing student life ('The rise of the rock dove'). The bird poems need reading and re-reading; the empathy is acute, but don't let that put you off – these poems aren't really about birds. And yet they are. Painful, witty, loving, long-sighted – I seem to be running out of adjectives. And no wonder.

the late U. A. Fanthorpe

…poems [that] remind those of us who write only in lists how much we need rhythm in our lives… A reminder of what really matters in this hectic world.

Sandi Toksvig

Also by Sue Vickerman

Poetry

Shag (Arrowhead Press 2003; Naked Eye Publishing 2017)
Kunst by 'Suki' (Indigo Dreams Publishing 2012)
Thin bones like wishbones by 'Suki' and Sue Vickerman
(Indigo Dreams Publishing 2013)
Adventus (Naked Eye Publishing 2017)

Fiction

Special needs (Cinnamon Press, Wales 2011)
A Small Life (Cinnamon Press, Wales 2012)
Two Small Lives (Naked Eye Publishing 2016)
True Life Nude (Naked Eye Publishing 2018)

Translated literature

Twenty Poems by Kathrin Schmidt (Arc Publications 2020)
It's over. Don't go there. Short stories, Kathrin Schmidt
(Naked Eye Publishing 2022)

Online fiction
asmalllife.co.uk
twosmalllives.co.uk
truelifenude.co.uk

Blog
sukithelifemodel.co.uk

The social decline of the oystercatcher

Sue Vickerman

Naked Eye Publishing

© Sue Vickerman 2005, 2022

First published 2005 by
Biscuit Publishing Ltd.

This edition published 2022 by
Naked Eye Publishing

All rights reserved

Book design and typesetting by Naked Eye
Cover illustration by Francesca Clayton

ISBN: 9781910981245

This book was written with support from Arts Council England
and the Scottish Arts Council

www.nakedeyepublishing.co.uk

Acknowledgements

Some of these poems previously appeared in *Coffee House, Orbis, Smiths Knoll, Mslexia, Acumen, The North, Review* (University of Leeds Alumni magazine, Issue 15, 2004), 'The Blue Room Anthology' (Diamond Twig 1999), 'The Litfest Poetry Competition Anthology' (Lancaster Litfest 2001). 'The rise of the rock dove' appears in 'Values in Higher Education', eds Simon Robinson and Clement Katulushi (Aureus Publishing 2005).

I would like to thank Bob Cooper and Jennifer Copley for their helpful comments on some of these poems; also my first editor Brian Lister at Biscuit Publishing, and for this new edition the Managing Editor of Naked Eye Publishing, Mike Kilyon. Further, I would like to acknowledge the support of the Scottish Arts Council in the completion of this collection.

THE SOCIAL DECLINE OF THE OYSTERCATCHER

For Friederike

Contents

The social decline of the oystercatcher.................15
Eiders.................16
Cormorant.................18
The black-backed gull.................19
Waiting for puffins.................20
Maintenance.................22
The sensitively thin bill of the shag.................23
Purple sandpiper.................24
Skylark.................25
Tate Gallery, Turner's unfinished room.................26
Portrait.................27
Wimpy Bar, Fraserburgh.................28
View of Lochnagar.................29
End of treatment.................30
Vigil, Drumnadrochit.................31
Your wedding.................32
The Commandos.................33
Borderline.................34
First time out.................35
Paula's funeral.................36
Low pressure.................37
Aberdeen Starbucks.................38
The millenium bed.................39
Victim.................40
Hearing about John Lennon.................41
Support work.................42
Infant Found In Rucksack At Bus Station.................43
Bedroom window.................44
Post-insemination.................45
Liesl's hens.................46
Boat woman.................48
Older women.................50
West Lake, Hangzhou.................51
Northern sights.................52
The rise of the rock dove.................54

First flurry of snow..56
Trelleborg to Sassnitz...57
Berlin Lichterfelde...58
December 24th...59
Between Christmas and New Year..60
Zarrentin..61

The social decline of the oystercatcher

Back then, you were the swaggering rocker
of wading birds; boldly-coloured, dazzling
in flight, the most conspicuous bird-of-shingle,
the loudest. I remember your effortless landings
on muddy sand-banks; your hot-shot red lenses;
how you eyed up the cockles. You always claimed
the most abundant mussel beds, the ones
on rocky outcrops in down-town estuaries,
the tangiest; always picked the best ridge of sand
for your high-tide roost. You were so cool
with your minimalist nest: no fuss – lay the eggs
on an exposed pebble shoal, let nature do the rest.

It was frequenting estuaries that brought you down.
Your stout, pale pink legs – not your best feature –
wandered too far in the long, dark winter. Increasingly
you nested by rivers, even on farmland, digging bluntly
in mud and soil when you used to be so at home
on rocky shores, on beaches. And thus it was

that your diet deteriorated from coastal molluscs
to earthworms. Now, even a good cockle year
doesn't bring you back. Instead you get into fights
over food. I've seen you poking through the rubbish
at night, spearing litter. I used to love watching you
on the beach, how you waited for a chance to strike
into an open shell, or simply hammered one free
with your powerful chisel-tipped bill.
But that was the coast, and this is now: not Norway,
not Iceland, but a long way up a northern river
with no shellfish. Only your clear, sharp
kleep voice tells me you're the same person.

Eiders

We said eleven at the estuary car-park,
out past that half-built estate,
past Mike and Helen's new flat
with the panoramas front and back.
We set off on Mike's walk, on dunes

staked out, he says, for the breeding season.
We all say it's freezing. Mike tells us
Helen's expecting. We mess up
the ski-slope of sand beside the roped-off
breeding ground, the hidden nests of terns.

Helen's striped jogging pants bat out
then furl. The stripes twist round and round
and round. Her lips are blue. Mike zips up
her front and pats it, and points out, up top,
the site of a church, the mound of its wall,

the swelling of a whole village buried
under the dune. Alone I wander over
to the rim of the cove where, on a slim peninsular,
the heavy female body of an eider
is nesting in a crevice

and I can't help staring at the turn
of her fat neck, her brown plainness,
her drooping flat head, the girders
of her legs beneath the barrow of her;
the heaviness of that motherly belly

so unlike the conspicuous black and whiteness
of the diving duck, his proud maleness,
how he shimmies with the others
on the rocks; how their feathers
point down their bills like arrows.

On the beach we eat bagels brought by Mike,
watching the eiders; how they squat in groups
like picnickers; how whole families of eiders
paddle in rock-pools, shellfish-hunting,
or run over the mud, or fly in long, low lines

across the bay on this cool day in April.
Mike hands out apples. We head for the cliffs
reminiscing about our fifteen-mile hikes.
The ascent is difficult. I glance at Helen
as Mike says, grinning, this is only the beginning.

Cormorant

We named birds while we waited.
At least the weather is good, I said,
as her blood ran out into the sun;
as the sea crept closer like a child.
A dark cloud came and went. A cormorant
struck up a reptilian posture, spectating
like a vulture. A seal sang, nonchalant.
Two fulmars landed heavily and swam
as we waved at the coxswain

who waved back, cutting the engine
as he passed the upward-angled bill
of the cormorant swallowing an eel,
neck kinked, elbows heraldic; as a girl
in a wetsuit jumped in and waded across;
as the lifeboat nosed into the shallows.

Last night I climbed back down to the rocks.
A jellyfish threaded with blood was flopped
in the gap where her foot must've twisted.
As I touched the tooth, the granite incisor
that ripped her, I heard the guttural laughter
of that lout, that good-for-nothing seabird
with the look of a set-down beer bottle
perched on a buoy, lazy-eyed, scanning about
for some poor fish to snap up and swallow.

The black-backed gull

After you'd gone, I returned to the beach one day
with a Tesco's bag, picked plastics out of the jaw
of the wide-mouthed cave, extracted bottles
from the line of chewed flotsam. Flies, disturbed
from seaweed nests, complained around my head
and a gannet came close then plunge-dived
between the waves rushing at my boots.

Finally all the unnatural colours were collected
in my carrier. Hearing a cry, I turned to face
the cove's dry throat and saw a Macdonalds-red
slit neck staining the bric-a-brac left by the tide,
the lemon-fizz bill of a puffin. I scanned the cliffs,
aimed rocks at the dog-bark of the murderous
black-backed gull: *Get away. Go. Get away.*

After restoring the cove to shades of grey,
to how it was with you, I heard the cry again
and, looking back, found myself whisker-close
to the past; to the hollow, widowed eyes of a seal.

Waiting for puffins

You said they would arrive in May.
Noticing a gossamer of droppings
cobwebbed over the cliffs, sheer rock
feathered into a duvet, my hopes soar
out of the window. I forfeit a cooked breakfast
for seaweed and scrambled pudding-stone,
locking the lighthouse but leaving a note
just in case: *Gone to puffins. You know where.*

Scanning the chess-board of sleek-backed auks
I train your loaned binoculars on profiles,
rubbing the steam of my hot look from your lenses,
trying to catch a distinctive beak, curious
eye-markings, tell-tale red among the grey suits
of kittiwakes. A thick-set fulmar hangs stiff-winged
on an updraught, stalls, then drops. Guillemots,
startled, unfurl overhead. I dodge, umbrella-ed.

Auks need ledges on which to rest, whereas puffins
dig burrows in the soft ground of cliff tops.

My boots catch on lichen, slip in pools
while the rising tide pulls slowly at the time
available, slides round another inlet. I clamber
beyond common sense, sure of a sighting,
the distinctively large head, the amusing waddle.
Scaling the milk-stained cliff among the waterfalls
of nests, I reach the final outcrop, and discover
an inaccessible bay, curved in a lipless smile.

There! I zoom in, breathless, on a patch like liquorice,
touching the focus lightly, waiting for a profile
that doesn't jab and point. I blink back salt,
blink away my double-vision, a thousand couplings.
But there are no bright, calypso beaks, jolly as plastic;
no sad-eyed, comical sea-birds from book-spines
and cartoons, the ones you promised; only auks'
dark looks and razorbills' blunt chins, and my eye-
corners lapped by the encroaching edge of the sea.

Maintenance

The man has come to scratch the pitch
from the lighthouse top. I file my nails.
Under the black is copper. I am rattled
off my window-seat by gale-force winds.
The boiler hums; I feel hot as snow drives
up the cliffs, smacks into his oilskin. Hard.
He is braced hard over the ball-shape.
He has tied himself to the dome, fixed
with a rope sufficient for anchoring ships.
He climbs to the tip, sets about the globe
of the weather-vane. It is February. A tanker slips
along the edge of the sea. The wind shakes salt
out of the sky. His lips are salt. He ducks
the batting arrow. One gust and he'll topple.

The sensitively thin bill of the shag

A squabble in the eaves, housemartins,
wakes us early. As I pour your breakfast tea
a gannet flop-glides off the lighthouse,
drops between smoke-rings of mist

while you swill spit from the basin,
put in your contacts, peer out at the tide
already lapping the slip-way, and I know
that you're going to shout *Heron! Let's go down.*

At the edge, where bladder-wrack stretches
skin-tight on the knees of boulders, where my boots
flatten pods and pick up slime, I remark
that the tide will isolate us if we're not careful

but you stride on, as usual, over thick kelp stipes,
shadows of fish in pools, liver-fleshed anemones,
and straddle the thin smile of a ravine, disregarding
the sea, how it foams your trainers into a wet shave,

how oystercatchers clack their knitting-needle beaks
like wives complaining, and herring gulls line up,
laddish, on ledges. Your interest is only in exotic visitors.
Whinchat you call over wave-noise. *Or maybe a wheat-ear.*

Meanwhile, on a rock cling-wrapped in jelly-fish,
a solitary shag lands in a shallow glide, his posture
less refined than a cormorant, his loosely-crested nape
spiked, rakish, brave against the dashing water

and I notice him looking me over in a way you never do.
Steep-browed, thin bill; fine hook at the tip. When I skid,
blushing, on mustard-smeared granite, he winks,
shows me his profile, flexing his seaweed wings.

Purple sandpiper

I lead you to the real beauties: brown
on beige, blue on blue like gulls' eggs,
or buffish, the eggs of the common tern
mottled with olive, the colours of Scotland.
After they dry they'll be as disappointing
as the slate-brown of a purple sandpiper.
But even as you speak, a wave shifts
more precious finds towards my toes.
They are too big for your pockets, too wet,
too heavy for the car. So I take snaps
of the best: pearl-skinned, unblemished
as the horizon, rough-smooth as your face.

Blue morning, November, another country.
When I hear the pack of photos drop in the hall,
pond-still, I turn to your beige pillow, slide
my hand through your chilled space, grey on grey.

Finally, in May, I purchase a book: slate-brown,
its pages the colour of bones. My beauties
will soon shimmer like a holiday, like treasure
rediscovered, in an album entitled 'Stones.'

Skylark

A shaken-out blanket of yellow rape
makes us pull up, picnic-minded. I laugh
as a comic-strip hare bounces into a field
nippled with cut turnips, but you miss it

and then on our backs in the rumpled meadow
I hear it first: the spiralling phrases,
the rising hover of the classic aerial singer,
piece of grit swimming over my eyeball,
a flicker in the chlorine sky. *Look*
I indicate the particle against the sun,
the speck on the blue screen of August

but you find the skylark sharp-tongued, shrill
as a kettle, its vibrato making you shiver,
sanding your sockets like migraine,
its ultimate plunge splitting your head.

Tate Gallery, Turner's unfinished room

I end up tired out, standing next to smeared areas
of white, feeling sick with the motion of his seas;
his massive canvas scratched all over like a girls' fight
to suggest the spray of breaking waves;
his sunrises too bright to stare into; the blaze
of his coastal light over the Isle of Thanet.

I back off from his dramatic handling of paint
and look onto the Thames from a triangular window,
onto the January city, realistically flat and grey
like wet newsprint slicked to a pavement

but behind my back, against the emulsion
I can feel him; the dynamism of flung paint,
his approaching storm, how it surges right up
to the frame's edges then crashes over.

Portrait

It took all day to get the backdrop right,
the perfect shot, that black-eyed look
behind the boat's sail, that dark light
that comes over at the approach
of a shower when the sun looks back
pulling a cloak after itself, when the ropes
turn silver, strung out like saliva;

morning til night, snapping the yacht's
unblinking portholes, blue awning,
folded tarpaulin, sail as brilliant
as an arctic tern's clean-tipped wing,
a rope like a serpent uncoiling,
fenders in teams, brass trim winking
at the apple cheek of a buoy

and Jim on deck in his boiler suit
reflecting on a knot in a figure-of-eight,
on a youth spent by the juke box
in the fish shop on the harbour,
on the yard where he first saw her,
on how he came to fall for
his Hillyard twelve-tonner.

He got more than he bargained for:
not just the fine figure of her
in bridal white against a midnight cloud;
not monochrome, but a rainbow,
hooked on her prow like ribbons.

Wimpy Bar, Fraserburgh

The sky a simple cut of cloth
down the length of the street; the sea
at the end, cupped between houses
like liquid metal. Salt drifts
on my table, sticks to my fleece

while the sharp-cornered sun
of the shortest day back-lights
the bus station; while the proprietor
stacks up dirties, wipes up sauce
and delivers my fish, battered.

A truck checks into the harbour.
A trawler, picked clean, gets in line
along the aluminium of a warehouse
where school-leavers in white
slap fish in sinks

as the tide turns, edges along the wall;
as tendrils of nets come alive in the water
and a boy with no home to go to
cracks open a padlock with a pebble,
slips into the rocking cradle of a boat

View of Lochnagar

I knew you would leave me.
I saw how your eyes climbed the map
at the Visitors' Centre, six miles to the top
of a mountain we hadn't planned on.

I said we didn't have the picnic for it,
nor the water. No sunhats. No sun-tan lotion
for that height. I was wearing tights
for god's sake, not hiking boots and socks

but your fingers played over the red sliver
of path, the numbered contours by the Falls
of the Glasallt. I could see the falls, a smear
on the chin of the mountain, way too far.

Our planned walk was on the level,
a simple circuit ribboning round the long loop of water
in cold sun, in air as fresh as ice.
I whipped out my camera, got a great shot

of a stag; of a rock half-tumbled then frozen
to the spot; of a treeless root; the scraped hyde
of the slope; the patches of heather burnt off;
you in your glasses like black holes, like the loch.

You left me at Glas-allt-Shiel,
at the shuttered-up lodge, that picnic spot
where the burn goes shallow and flat and
rolls out like a pebble carpet to meet Loch Muick.

I knew straight away you'd set off for the summit,
for that elusive view of Lochnagar. So I got out
my sketchbook, looked up at the mountain and drew it.
I'd have hung it in the hall, if you'd liked it.

End of treatment

After the long, dark winter,
the many samples taken out of you
and poured away, the last appointment
at the centre, the hard facts,
we take to the coast in pouring rain
for a difficult walk on sliding shale,
dodging pebbles that bounce back at us
when we try to fling them as far as the water

and you comment on the
womb-like quality of rock pools,
their dark wetness, their walls
lined with the red mess of anemones
that retract inside themselves when touched;
tight-nubbed clots that shrink
into crevices, shutting out predators,
blood-coloured and yet bloodless.

Vigil, Drumnadrochit

The first of Britain's 21st century engagements in war triggered many local protest vigils

It was almost time. Night wavered over the green
like chimney smoke as the village's inhabitants
drifted from snickets and gates in the final minutes,
not in droves, like sheep, but in ones,
alone as prophets, leaving the established paths,
congregating by a bench more fit for picnics

where a woman in woollens handed out candles
with a muffled smile to the Free Church pastor;
the postmaster; students home for their breaks;
two plumpish young mums who jiggled their prams
and fussed; a Japanese tourist, newly off the bus
from Inverness who ambled over, curious.

The vigil commenced with a struck match. A cruel
thorny frost crowned its head. Fingers flared red,
passing the flame between cold, cupped hands.
I was in the East during Vietnam, I saw the soldiers'
faces. It's not about Saddam. What do people
in Japan think about the possibility of war?

When the cold got to us, we marched to the obelisk
in the shadow of the looming distillery, counted
on the list nine McDonald men among the lives
laid down, iced-over; stamped our feet, chanting
our opposition, the glen echoing our attempt
to circulate blood like the sound of distant artillery.

Your wedding
for Jochen and Sylvie

I don't expect big hats with veils
or anything as English as a rain-shower
during the photographs, waiting for hours
in the wet while the bride is posed this way
then that. Flowers, yes: white wild-flowers
woven through Sylvie's midnight hair like stars,
and a handsome knight, and a dress like Rapunzel's
that catches on briars as it trails through the forest
like the gowns they wore in Grimm's Fairytales.

I have doodled your wedding into a rosebud
on my June page, petalled like peace-graffiti
around the dentist, Mum and Dad's anniversary,
coach for rally leaves Market Square seven thirty.
But my calendar is battle-scarred, the start-date
plotted in red felt-tip; skirmishes down my margins;
the day the people cheered the departing ship;
the missiles that landed among civilians, bleeding
through the paper like poppies in their millions.

When the radio forecasts the weather then forecasts
the next gain, when heavy bombing makes better copy
than heavy rain, when the ratings on fairytale romance
are down because action-adventure is the current rage
and the dead child lies blood-stained across the page,
your marriage is a cottage in the woods, a haven;
and when holy war wins more viewers than holy union
and altars are looted, and love affairs across the nation
falter, your wedding is a peace demonstration.

The Commandos

The hills at Achnacarry interleave like drinkers' hands
slapped in a pile on the bar, sworn comrades.
From 1942 these lands were the training ground
of grim-faced men who swaggered through peat bogs
in steel boots and berets; who would jut their chins
at a profiled stag, and point their low-slung rifles
at Ben Nevis and its cowering side-kick Aonach Mor.

You came expecting a landscape of action-adventure:
Das Schottische Hochland mentioned chieftains
and kilted lairds. Standing in mud you trace the statistics,
picture that beach in France, your face crumpling
at the beauty of lichen flowering on the torsos
of the three weathered lads, copper-jowled friends
who'd die for each other, three pals on a plinth

above a valley that ripples like Alsace with the stands
of Learnachan Forest, where a grouse rises territorially
above shrapnel-peppered tips of larches, where mist
snags on gleaming spikes of pines like a cigarette pall.
This is fighting men's terrain, under this wide white flag
of cloud. You retreat into the dark woods, make it back
to the car-park before the imminent outbreak of rain.

Borderline

Leaving the A7 we nose after a tanker up the valley
like Matchbox toys on the mound of a parent's belly.
Scotland's lowlands lie shivering, bare as the body
of a northern nudist; hairless, bluish-skinned.

Near Gretna Green your arm falls to my thigh
after a gear-change as we take a narrow bend
around the hillock of an ankle and discuss idly, again,
whether or not to get married in some sense

while great pillows of night loom over the motorway
and the light fails. We cruise a lazy leg towards the peak
of a sharp hip propped against the sky, then dip
into the vale of a folded arm, and see, at last, England's

green counterpane thrown over the island. You exhale
admiration for the patchwork of my homeland drawn up
to the road, and list the things you love: the armies of mills
on the skyline, stiff upper lips, the queen, rain on the hills,

afternoon teas. But I point out the boundaries – the way
sheep seethe like maggots on the sectioned-off terrain.
See how the whole body floating in its own polluted sea
is diseased; look at this armpit we've slipped into.

First time out

Pausing for breath in Toxteth in a sea wind
you say you feel better. Last week's headlines
from the Echo unreel along derelict streets,
it's almost a movie except that the sky
is not painted, static. We watch it
slipping over itself like an oil-slick
gliding down-river, until you stop, look:

on a bench outside The Angel, women
without men play cards, flick ash, keep watch
on their buggies, give slaps. We catch the stench
of endless last rounds, lock-ins on dark nights,
then you frown, pull my arm, point
at the tar by your foot where a baby bird lies
cheek down, ribbed with bike tyres.

From the bricked-up church a chipped saint
is reaching out like a Big Issue seller
but beyond the brewery you see a bright stage-set
and we pass him by, hurry on to our destination,
strung-out lights, galleries, the marina where palms
wave from balconies and clustered yachts
chatter like extras. I toss change in a busker's hat
and get us icecreams, first of the season.

You know, we could move here if you wanted.
But the sky pulls you down, down to the edge of the quay
where a rail weathered to a hairgrip is all that keeps you
from the mud of the empty Mersey.
You remark on the beauty of distant lace-necked cranes
while I sense rain, notice pockmarks on the water's skin
and although you're smiling, I do up your coat.
You know we shouldn't stand here for very long.

Paula's funeral

As *Woman's Hour* ends you indicate left
for a small coastal town, suggest we break the drive,
avoid arriving early at the crem and having to chat.

We cut through on B-roads. The sea
is unemotional, dead flat. We park,
walk back to where the gift shops start,

stop short in a tearoom doorway faintly rainbowed
like a memory, hearing the strains
of Classic FM, watching the schoolgirl waitress

sponging jam from her apron; the people conversing
right through Elgar's emotional piece for violin,
drinking their tea, not listening.

Low pressure

I said it would be stern as a school uniform,
dull as winter heather. But Aberdeen was gentle
as an egg-box, pencil-shaded, hesitant outlines
smudged by the weather, cock-eyed sea-birds perched
on cardboard cut-out turrets high above the shops
on Union Street while heads wrapped up like sweets
bobbed by and men strode down to the gaudy ships

where you, delighted, took snaps of the docks,
metallic red and blue blocked into sketched space.
I could live here, you said, lingering at the sight
of a papery warehouse blown empty. That night
on the coast road we parked under lowering cloud
and argued, while behind us in fading light, the city
mulched like papier-mâché beneath the press of granite.

Aberdeen Starbucks

A' these beggars, he nods through the glass
at Union Street, *they started off on the rigs.*
Across the road, a pair of knickers waves
from the spire of a nightclub made from a church.
*Made megabucks as roustabouts, then spent it a'
oan sex and drugs. Load o' junkies, now.*
Cream from a tall cappuccino scurfs his lip.
Canna buy ye another o' those?

Dead grounds knock into bins in time
with the jazz track, as he calls back from the bar,
Ae, Billy, wis tha' a grandy latty? as milk
spits from aluminium taps, *Willa put chocolate
oan toap?* as Nina Simone croons, as the rain
slacks off, as oil execs leave their offices
by taxi, as down the road the homeless
leave the day-centre like one big family.

The millenium bed

is vacant, unmade.
Cardboard sheet. Naked brick.
Packing-case. Fish-crate base.
Patch of nosebleed. Road grit.
Tarpaulin. Pigeon feathers.
Mogadons. Not so much a futon
as a bed made in Britain

yet this bed, though indigenous,
is not suited to the climate.
Just as a Japanese mattress
needs a dry environment
to adequately air, this bed
needs a roof to keep out moisture,
and some kind of wind-breaker,

also a sound-barrier between itself
and the rest of the car-park.

Victim

So I took Brian's hand
after he'd washed the blood off it
and he led me to a tenement on Castlegate.
The tug on my arm was a child's or an old man's.
It turned out in court he was twentyeight.

The thing to look at was in the basement.
The other flats had nets in rags or blankets
instead of curtains. One had a Union Jack.
I flagged up an idea – Brian,
would you like to stay out here?

but he led me down a nineteen-seventies swirly carpet
to a place where people had been to the toilet,
me in my summer skirt (outside it was glorious).
Sure enough, the blood all around us
matched the stuff on Brian's shirt.

Have I killed him? he asked. We stood and looked
at a breeze-block the size of a white sliced loaf,
thick with jam, beside the bashed-in brains
of a man in vest and trousers.
I went through the motions of taking the pulse

then nodded, watching Brian's face
turn yellow like wallpaper getting older.
Don't worry, I patted his shoulder,
him looking like his life was over,
me holding out my tobacco.

Hearing about John Lennon

The gig went well. Just after midday
he gets up, a bit hungry, hung-over.
Halfway through licking a Rizla, stops dead,
catching the headline again at the end:
a single shot, two sons left and Yoko's in shock,
she was there.

Yoko was there.
The shock of it. A single shot. Two sons left.
Catching the headline again at the end
he stops dead, halfway through licking a Rizla,
hung over, a bit hungry, just out of bed,
just after midday, when the gig had gone so well.

Support work

You have me kneeling, working the back of your head.
Your hair-straightener's red hot, but then goes dead.

You were ripped off to the tune of a tenner. Worse,
you only found out after that it wasn't lifted from Jessops

but out of another girl's flat while she was off her head,
and even worse, that girl's now dead

although on the other hand she won't miss it

Infant Found In Rucksack At Bus Station

It was eight pounds something
and merited a paragraph: *Girl
bunked off maths to give birth
in recycling bin near swimming baths.*

Three days passed before she admitted it.
In all the fuss over who should have it –
the next adoptive couple on the waiting list
or the new grandma, who put in a bid

after meeting with a reporter; after all
it was her miracle granddaughter –
a new twist got headlines across the nation
for one night only: *Baby Death Shock*.

In the aftermath, after the whole thing
had died down (was it a nurse who dropped it
then hopped it?), the brave young mum
did an HNC in Administration.

Bedroom window

That's the sun.
Hot. Hot.

Those are clouds,
those milky heaps
like yoghurt,
like the cumulus
of sheets piled high
at the end of your cot.

Sleep, now. Sleep
in the un-ironed sky.

Post-insemination

After the clinic we picnic to celebrate.
Once inside a uterus, you say,
there's no escape: it's life or death,
sink or swim. You show me one in a million
midges breast-stroking for the enamel rim
of your cup; point out the lips of a fish
breaking the membrane of the water's surface;
the ant latching onto the biscuit crumb

but I only see how the sun streams down,
sparkling, liquid, yet sizzles into nothing
on the hard steel panel of the lake.

Liesl's hens

I am, and have always been, a plain brown hen
with no name. So was my sibling. We were tame.
We had the odd bad habit. So what, if I bit her chest
until she was bald, and she did the same?
We did what mattered. We laid. We laid and laid.

In the yard, in the very corner into which she last scuttered,
stand the New Hampshires, the importeds, silk-cravatted,
superior; the ones with pet names. They shake
their feathery slippers at me, preen each other's heads,
while behind the house, leaning rakish against the bricks

is a red-lipped axe, and in the kitchen, blood
spots the tiles like Smarties. I fold my wings in prayer,
seeing my sibling's neck in Liesl's fist, how she lifts
an elbow to pluck his armpit; picks
the last feather from his groin, a final hair

from his belly, collecting the bits on a kitchen-roll,
de-pilling my sibling like washed-out knitting.
Soon, on the stainless-steel drainer, two kidneys
and a liver; yellow-topped heart flopped in a bowl
while the children crouch near the buckets, waiting

as Liesl snips the string of my sibling's ankles,
waiting to snatch those daffy feet and run,
just like their father, who learnt the art of slaughter
from doing in rabbits, who slipped my sibling's
tousle-topped brain like a trinket into the bin.

In the yard, the New Hampshires pirouette, shake out
their elegant tails, pretty-pretty. I sit down quickly to hide
my chickeny legs. So what if your eggs are a bigger size?
They are far less frequent. And how dare you giggle,
knowing I've watched a preview of my own demise?

Your colours are garish, your lipsticked peckers insane,
your slippers ridiculous. I wish when you first came
we'd never offered the sound advice which we didn't heed
ourselves: *don't be nice. Don't offer your head for a scratch
or a pat, or you could end up without it. Don't be tame.*

Boat woman

For all women living alone or together on boats

I gave up everything for the swan's neck
of a tiller bar, the liquorice whiff
of a canal basin; for life in a wharf

or along a cut; for lines of willows,
a boat nosing in like a curious dog,
the slippage of litter beneath the bows,
the hollow smell of a packhorse bridge
like the cellars of palaces, brass bands
practising in the mill buildings, peaceful fish;

for drips that pluck the water's skin like kisses,
frilled-out skirts of engine oil, the touch
of a reed – light as a cat's whisker; blackbirds
in sycamores, tangles of rushes, trains
in tunnels, a panicking moorhen, ducks
snapping up sliced bread, a works siren.

I gave up everything because I was
too weak, or too strong, whereas here
the worst that can happen is a bed-spring
jammed round my rudder, or a shopping trolley
wedged right under. Here, all it takes
if things go wrong is a jolly good dollop

of engine grease. Here, it's me who decides
what's what. I can leave the dishes, live
on biscuits, tip my piss-pot over the side,
hop onto the towpath and pick brambles
in a margarine carton, paint the kitchen
tangerine with purple spots; move on

from these frayed edges at the backs
of houses – their bald lawns, their compost,
their unclipped hedges, dismantled units,
cement in sacks; a toilet, laid out; carcasses
of barbecues, this patio left unfinished
due to divorce, this mess of kitchen waste.

They stare in through my boat's fish-eye:
the joggers, the dogwalkers, the child
on his father's shoulders asking why
as I lift the weed hatch in the engine room,
reach in as far as my armpit, pull out
that dead duck by the rope of its neck

with satisfaction, enjoying the simple action
of freeing my propeller of muck and plastic.
I smile at them; no, I sing as I swill my boat off
with a bucket, as I rig up my hammock
on the well deck from the washpole socket
to the handrail; as I float off, swinging.

Older women
a response to 'Men' by Kate Clanchy

I love their skin, crazed as an old dish,
their scent like freshly printed literature,
herb pillows, denim gone soft in the wash;
how they chop wood, take nostalgia trips
to Greenham, lift bikes up steps, do weights,
knit socks. I love the glimpse of private space
between shirt and skin, slacks on firm hips
from climbing in France. Women who drink Guinness
and wear rainbow woollies from Brazil, and embrace
other women; women whose positions on sex
are as relaxed as armchairs; women whose exes
are shelved in albums. They'll grab you like cake,
light your candles, lead you to believe,
then smile, put on their cycle clips and leave.

West Lake, Hangzhou
for Sheng Jie Hua

The day before my flight we cycle
to your favourite spot on borrowed bikes,
beyond that ridge of hills, out past the Temple
of the Soul's Retreat, the Silk Museum,
the Dragon's Cave, another pagoda,
stopping at last in a flap of skirts
on the ornamental elbow of a bridge
where the lake is said to be clearest –

though it's not what you promised: not like glass,
not green tea, but cold coffee filmed over,
cigarette ends passing under like boats. So we
cycle on to Autumn Moon On Calm Lake
where the magnolias are said to be idyllic;
me behind, loving your blouse of cherry trees
and orioles; your hat, flipped off, dancing
on elastic; your hair done up with a plastic lotus.

This is how I'll remember you:
these slim-hipped willows, this picnic
at Three Pools Mirroring The Moon,
these long legs of bamboos, these leaves
fingering my neck; that woman in white,
resting her paddles like a butterfly; that punt
splintering off from the jetty as we say goodbye,
how it slips into the skin of the lake.

Northern sights
for a German friend after he was blinded

I Manchester Airport

I planned to tell you about the turbanned men
reading The Times while waiting; a Jamaican
in charge of the catering, Hasidic Jews
flocked at the Lunn Poly stand,
an espresso bar where bacon slivers
visible along the cutline of baguettes
don't smell at all, though in fact this
is England where we eat bacon for breakfast.
But your stick tap-dances over my rehearsal,
avoiding objects, except that you say
coffee smells the same, and I accept
that the rush of air as you landed was universal
and our rain will have more effect on your stay
than the promise of an Indian take-away.

II Beer

Your cheeks are glass. The storm dashes down
the dale, down your face until you perceive
the moor like a skylight, thrashed with sleet.
Arriving at the Old Silent, drowned,
you turn down a pint. I buy a round
for one. Your salad arrives un-dressed,
so English, but in the end, lettuce is lettuce,
drifting from your fork without a sound,
fluttering from your plate to the ground.
Heading home on the bus your reflection
still shines wet. I change the subject, ask
whether anything else leads you to believe
that this is England. Sheep, you say.
Later, I order an Indian take-away.

III Curry

I try to empathise, dutifully,
suffer that violent red-green lightshow
in your head, but I see a rainbow,
and say nothing as it fades beautifully
like the line of your cheek against green
as we passed wild garlic, or when I saw
the fell glowing red behind your jaw.
You gasp, sharp as a lens zooming in,
tasting Madras, a gentle fold of nan bread
in your hands. For now, I'll turn your head
with picked lilac, but later I'll persuade you
to spend autumn here: sit close
to the fire, taste coal, feel twilight crocheted
round the village, smell northern dusk.

The rise of the rock dove
to mark the centenary of the University of Leeds

To my fledgling eye, Leeds was red-brick gullies,
crew-cut hedges, hard-faced trees, parks with frayed edges.
Today, when I glide in on an InterCity intending to visit
old roosts, I find instead chrome balconies, palms
waving from penthouses, sandblasted ledges

but there among the slender backs of bright tower-blocks
I spot some old-timers, the elderly chimneys along the canal
which haven't smoked since the fifties and look well on it;
the Town Hall in its helmet, and across from the jail's
tough nut, that monocled brain-box, the Parkinson clock.

It was hard, being part of the first pigeon influx.
Today when I hop on a Headingley bus
there are no second glances, yet I lived on campus
in times when pigeons received dirty looks; were dismissed
as chancers; were not even mentioned in certain bird-books.

We were treated by some as if we weren't birds at all.
But I was there for the transformation (some would say 'fall')
when we flocked in from pit towns, bog-standard quarries
and council tips to take up scholarships; created myths
of our past as 'rock doves' with a wild rural ancestry.

We were the first to wear nondescript colours
and hooded tops. We had red-eyed good looks
(if you like that type), but were written off by some
as scruffs, compared to those beautiful species
down south who resided in spires and turrets.

Yet we pigeons, though ordinary, though not all
the highest of flyers, had guts: we were the ones
who spoke out; the loud, feral townies. We taught
the southerners how to strut; how to conduct
their courtship displays on the Parkinson steps,

how not to be ruffled by complaints about squats
on the Great Hall's frontage, or the corrosive effects
of droppings. Soon, white streaks were as symbolic
as raised fists, and are now compared by sociologists
to the raised white streaks of self-harmed wrists

but see how our ways have been hijacked:
how other birds now scavenge for the best pickings,
flock into bars, get caught mating on shopfronts,
fly home at weekends. Meanwhile, ethnic pigeons
are wearing Nike to disguise their origins.

It's all a far cry from when we colonised Leeds 6,
rode bikes, picked through skips, shook buckets
to collect for the pickets, ate veggie, spent nights
doing soup-runs from St George's Crypt, marched
for other people's rights. We have been tamed,

pigeon-holed, allotted our place in the pecking order.
We have better-feathered nests; our status
is above the rest; our ethnicity has the respected
name and face of 'rock dove'. But remember this:
no bird-book, to this day, gives pigeons proper space.

First flurry of snow

skittering across
the window pane like ghost ants
leaving an ice grave

it lands on the grass
a necklace spilled off its thread
fake pearls that won't last

Trelleborg to Sassnitz

The radar of a small green lighthouse is spinning
across my porthole. You beckon me out to the deck, point
at a tousle of windmills on the headland as we dock
alongside the dark sinew of somewhere that isn't Dover,
the unwinding snake of another foreign territory.

In the phone-booth of the terminal, I clutch the faint question
in the receiver picking with difficulty through currency
in your uncurling fist. Salt-lipped you shift your rucksack
while the digital seconds flicker out, and my answer
no we're not in Berlin; not yet, gets cut to a single negative.

Berlin Lichterfelde

Behind us, the eastern outskirts.
Beyond us, the fence where the border was
and the evening stretching empty
into the heart of the country.

These hard frosts would sometimes last all day.
I used to count lights in the tower blocks
of that Stalinist housing complex.
There were deer, before the new highway.

That couple walking their dogs
are in the area where the mines were.
Imagine watch-towers along this track.
They'd get out of their patrol cars to chat and urinate,

machine guns pulling on their shoulders.
Imagine hearing the order, seeing another man
run for the border like that dog off its lead
running for the trees. Imagine obeying it.

December 24th

It is almost five. It is *Heiligabend*.
The forecast shows snow cartwheeling over Saarland.
The sun goes down on your cul-de-sac,
on your parents' small, well-tended garden.

Your yard is swept. Your steps are gritted.
Your mother's broom rests in an apple tree's elbow.
She hurries outdoors at the very last minute
to dead-head a rose.

Your father is on the point of lighting
the candles on a tree dug out of the Saar Basin
which, from the plane, glittered
like a Christmas card.

You have always told me how the waiting
was hard; was the best thing of all: how,
when the bells finally toll across the valley,
the whole village feels holy.

Between Christmas and New Year

I woke up in a fog like flannelette,
came out of the crook of my elbow
thinking I was in England, seeing the milk-bottle blue
whiteness through the glass, the way sheets
fill back yards in late December.
The train was at a halt.
The sign read *Idar-Oberstein*
in tall, bent script like piano fingers

and I glimpsed, below the famous cliffs, the town's outline
when the fog swished back then drew closed –
not pretty like the postcards, but caught off-guard
with that feeling of emptiness that lingers
around the end of the season.

We began slipping out of the station
and I caught you in the double-glazing, smiling
for no reason, smiling right through me so sadly.

Zarrentin

I remember the deathly silence afterwards,
how flat the land was, a scribble
of poplars, pencil-sketched bushes,
the blank look of a lake in December,
sky like a drawn-down blind
as high and wide as a Suffolk winter

but this was Zarrentin, six hours
before the end of the year;
a muddle of trees, a twisted puzzle
of a root, a leafless bush –
one last red berry in its claw like a pill,

a weekender from Hamburg
power-walking, shattering ice lids
from the tops of puddles; the special issue
dropped from his rucksack
as he sprinted into the distance
before I could call him back,

leaving me with the English princes,
tanks in a line, a lottery-winning family,
a child's distended belly, a soldier's grin

and the nakedness of a tree
lying where it fell beneath the weight
of disused nests, the rotting stomach
of a rowing boat dragged out of the lake
and upturned, the dried-blood smell
of mushrooms on carcasses

and still there's time: it hasn't happened yet;
and the sharp, ugly phrases of ducks.

Naked Eye Publishing
A fresh approach

Naked Eye Publishing is an independent not-for-profit micropress intent on publishing quality poetry and literature with a particular focus on translation. We aim to take a midwife role in facilitating the translation of works that have until now been disregarded by English-language publishing. We will be happy if we function purely as an initial stepping-stone both for overlooked writers and first-time literary translators.

Each of us at Naked Eye is a volunteer, competent and professional in our work practice, and not intending to make a profit for the press. We see ourselves as part of the revolution in book publishing, embodying the newly levelled playing field, sidestepping the publishing establishment to produce beautiful books at an affordable price with writers gaining maximum benefit from sales.

nakedeyepublishing.co.uk

www.ingramcontent.com/pod-product-compliance
Lightning Source LLC
Chambersburg PA
CBHW071800080526
44588CB00013B/2311